LUKE LITTLER

■SCHOLASTIC

Published in the UK by Scholastic, 2025
Scholastic, Bosworth Avenue, Warwick, CV34 6UQ
Scholastic Ireland, 89E Lagan Road, Dublin Industrial Estate, Glasnevin, Dublin, D11 HP5F

SCHOLASTIC and associated logos are trademarks and/or
registered trademarks of Scholastic Inc.

Text © CWLA Agency, 2025
Cover illustration © Alan Brown, 2025
Inside illustrations on pages 25, 37 & 143 © Adobe, 2025

The moral rights of the author and illustrator have been asserted by them.

ISBN 978 0702 34427 5

A CIP catalogue record for this book is available from the British Library.

All rights reserved.
This book is sold subject to the condition that it shall not, by way of trade or otherwise, be lent, hired out or otherwise circulated in any form of binding or cover other than that in which it is published. No part of this publication may be reproduced, stored in a retrieval system, or transmitted in any form or by any other means (electronic, mechanical, photocopying, recording or otherwise), or used to train any artificial intelligence technologies without prior written permission of Scholastic Limited. Subject to EU law, Scholastic Limited expressly reserves this work from the text and data-mining exception.

Printed in the UK
Paper made from wood grown in sustainable forests and other controlled sources.

10 9 8 7 6 5 4 3 2 1

Scholastic does not have any control over and does not assume any
responsibility for any third-party websites or other platforms, or their content.

www.scholastic.co.uk

For safety or quality concerns:
UK: www.scholastic.co.uk/productinformation
EU: www.scholastic.ie/productinformation

CONTENTS

THE MAKING OF A SUPERSTAR 7
TALK THE TALK 16
RULES OF THE GAME 26
CHOOSE YOUR ARROWS 36
THROWING SKILLS AND TECHNIQUES 41
LITTLERMANIA 44
FROM TODDLER TO WORLD CHAMPION 48
AT A GLANCE: LUKE'S SENSATIONAL 2024! 55
HITTING THE BULLSEYE 60
2025 PDC WORLD DARTS CHAMPIONSHIP 61
RECORD BREAKER! 70
THE WORLD OF DARTS 74
SPLITTING THE ARROW 77
WORLD DARTS COUNCIL (WDC) 79

PROFESSIONAL DARTS CORPORATION (PDC)	80
WORLD DARTS FEDERATION (WDF)	82
PDC WOMEN'S SERIES	88
PDC TOUR CARD	90
ORDER OF MERIT	93
TIMELINE OF LITTLER'S CAREER HIGHLIGHTS	102
LUKE IN 2025 AND GOING FORWARD...	111
LUKE'S 2025 PREMIER LEAGUE DARTS JOURNEY	114
THROWING FOR FUN	122
A BRIEF HISTORY OF DARTS	127
WOMEN IN DARTS	133
LUKE LITTLER TIMELINE	135
BEYOND 2025	142
IT'S ALL IN THE NAME	144
WORLD CHAMPION DARTS QUIZ	146

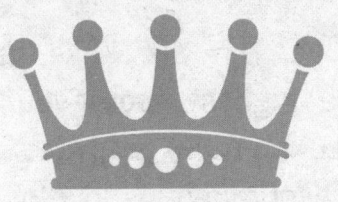

THE MAKING OF A SUPERSTAR

Calling all darts fans and those new to the sport! If you're wondering how an ordinary lad from Warrington became an overnight internet sensation and one of the greatest darts players in the world, then keep turning the pages to discover the amazing facts and stats about the phenomenal Luke 'The Nuke' Littler.

At the tender age of just 18 months, while still in nappies, Luke loved throwing toy darts at a magnetic board that his dad had bought him. Was this a sign of the path he was to take?

By the time he was six, Luke had scored his first 180 – the highest score you can get with three darts! Luke's mum and dad, spotting their son's talent, encouraged his love of the game and took him to their local pub to play and practise every week. He joined the St Helens Darts Academy around the age of nine and was so good that he could compete in the under-21 darts leagues, winning titles and showcasing his skills.

"I told everyone I was actually in nappies when I started playing. I'm not sure they believed me."

His first major break, and one that was to be a significant milestone in launching his meteoric career, came in 2021, when the then 14-year-old Luke won his first senior title at the Irish Open. This earned him a place to compete in the 2022 World Darts Federation (WDF) World Darts Championship.

The next few years were to change the course of Luke's life, culminating in his sensational win in January 2025 at the biggest darts competition in the world – the Professional Darts Corporation (PDC) World Darts Championship – just a couple of weeks before his 18th birthday. By beating three-time world champion Michael van Gerwen 7–3, Luke became the youngest person ever to win this competition.

Aged 17, and already a world champion, Luke set out on what promised to be an incredible career. Luke's dream is to win every major darts title at least once. His humble journey is a powerful and motivating reminder of the rewards one can achieve with hard work, dedication and passion. Now that's a real, **"One hundred and eighty-y-y-y-y-y!"**

DID YOU KNOW?

Luke loves to get a doner kebab – meat, lettuce and loads of mayo – at the end of every match!

'THE NUKE' FILES

NAME: Luke Littler

NICKNAME: the Nuke

DATE OF BIRTH: 21 January 2007

ZODIAC SIGN: Aquarius

PLACE OF BIRTH: Runcorn, England

PARENTS: Lisa and Tony Littler

SCHOOL: Padgate Academy

FAMOUS FOR: becoming the youngest-ever world darts champion after winning the 2025 World Darts Championship, just before his 18th birthday.

LITTLERMANIA: Luke's rise to fame led to an increased uptake in interest in the sport, especially from young people, dubbed the "Luke Littler effect".

FOOTBALL TEAM: Luke is a Manchester United Fan. He has supported them since 2013.

RUGBY TEAM: Luke supports his local rugby league team, the Warrington Wolves.

DID YOU KNOW?

Luke's 'walk-on' music to games is the song *Greenlight* by Pitbull, featuring Flo Rida and Lunchmoney Lewis. Luke has loved the song since he was a child. He was an avid fan of WWE wrestling and attended a WWE Wrestlemania event in the USA with his dad when he was 10 years old. This was where he heard the song. Luke said in an interview with *The Sun* newspaper, "I thought that if I did make it – I was playing football at the time a little bit – then that would be my walk-on song." Well, he didn't make it in football, but he is certainly making it in the world of darts!

THE NUKE

Luke's darts nickname, 'The Nuke', reflects his explosive talent and his ability to dominate matches with his exciting game playing techniques, which other players respect and his fans absolutely love!

INSPIRATION

Students at Luke's old school, Padgate Academy, have been inspired by Luke's success, which shows that anything is possible with practice, resilience and determination. There has been a surge in interest in the school's darts club.

"I'll keep what I've been doing — in the morning I will have a ham and cheese omelette, then a pizza for lunch. That's what I have done every day."

– Luke's pre-match routine

TALK THE TALK!

If you don't know your oche from your big fish yet, fear not! The world of darts has its own extensive slang, full of strange terms that are downright confusing for those who aren't fluent in talking the darts talk. Check out this comprehensive glossary of darts terms to get you started. Learning the language will help you feel part of the darts world and will impress your fellow darts players.

Arrows: the actual darts you throw. If someone says, "Great arrows!" they are impressed with your score.

Bag of nails: throwing three single 1s with all three of your darts in a single 'visit' – your turn at the board.

Bail out: hitting a high triple with your last dart after having scored a low number with your first two darts.

Barrel: the main part of the dart, which is held when throwing.

Bed: each specific segment on a dartboard.

Bed and Breakfast: when you score 26 points in one visit, usually with a single 20, a single 5 and a single 1. A very, very long time ago, staying at a bed and breakfast would have only cost you two shillings and six pence (which was said as two and six)!

Big Fish: scoring a 170 checkout (triple 20, triple 20 and a bullseye). This is the biggest possible finish with three darts. The bullseye, usually worth 50, counts as a double 25.

Bounce Out: when your dart falls out of the board.

Bullseye: the red centre circle on a dartboard, worth 50 points.

Bull Out: winning the game by hitting the bullseye.

Champagne Breakfast (also known as the Grand Slam): hitting a triple 20, a triple 5 and a triple 1 in one visit (a triple 'bed and breakfast'!).

Checkout: the score that wins the game. It must be finished on a double in one visit.

Clock: the dartboard itself (it looks a bit like the face of a clock).

Double top: the double 20.

Double trouble: when the player can't hit the double needed to win a game.

Downstairs: the lower section of a dartboard.

Feathers or flights: the wings at the end of a dart that help it fly in a straight trajectory.

Game on: said by the referee to start the game.

Game, shot: said by the referee after a player wins the match.

Hat-trick: hitting the bullseye with all three darts in one turn.

Leg: a single game of 501 played within a match. Most professional matches are made up of a number of sets. Each set is split into legs.

Madhouse: finishing the game on a double 1.

Nine-darter: the perfect leg of darts using just nine darts to get from 501 to 0.

Oche (pronounced OCK-ee): the line the players stand behind when they throw their darts. Also called the 'throw line' or the 'toe line'.

One-hundred-and-eighty: three darts inside the triple 20 segment, making a score of 180. This is the highest score possible in one visit. When a player achieves this, the match announcer usually shouts out, in a sing-song voice, *"One hundred and eightyyyyy!"* and the members of the audience cheer loudly, jump in the air and wave signs.

DID YOU KNOW?
Darts players have been using darts slang since the early 1900s when the game began to grow in popularity in the UK. Many of the catchy words came from the pubs and clubs where most darts games were played. The slang continues to evolve with the modern game.

DID YOU KNOW?
The oche line is 2.37 m (7 ft and 9 ¼ in) away from the front of the dartboard.

DID YOU KNOW?
The bullseye is often called a 'cork'.

Set: a particular number of legs to win. The first player to win a majority of those legs wins the set. For example, a set might be the best of three legs. The first to win two legs wins the set.

Shanghai: when you hit the single, double and triple of the same segment in one turn.

Spider: the wiring on the face of the dartboard which divides the segments.

Three in a bed: three darts in the same number.

Ton: a score of 100 points.

Tops: the double 20 on the dartboard.

Upstairs: the upper section of a dartboard.

Visit: a turn in the game, when you throw three darts.

Woody: a shot when a dart lands outside the scoring zone.

ONE HUNDRED AND EIGHTYYYYY!

2024 was a great year for Luke. Across all of his tournaments for the calendar year, he hit 836 180s, smashing the previous record set in 2022 by Michael Smith who hit 714.

FACT

NINE-DARTER PERFECT LEG

A nine-darter is a perfect scoring game of 501. Getting a nine-darter is a rare event, so much so that it is known as a 'perfect leg'. Getting a perfect leg requires an incredible amount of skill, precision and concentration, as a player must finish the leg of 501 in just nine darts. For example, they could score three triple 20s (180 points), followed by another three triple 20s (180 points) and finishing with a triple 20 (60 points), a triple 19 (57 points) and a double 12 (24).

FACT

In major tournaments a cash prize is usually given for achieving a nine-darter. At the age of 18, Luke Littler had already achieved six professional nine-dart legs!

1. **Bahrain Darts Masters**, 19 January 2024, against Nathan Aspinall.

2. **Players Championship 1** (Wigan), 12 February 2024, against Michele Turetta.

3. **Belgian Darts Open final**, 10 March 2024, against Rob Cross.

4. **Premier League Darts final**, 23 May 2024, against Luke Humphries.

5. **Players Championship 5** (Leicester), 11 March 2025, against Adam Hunt.

6. **Premier League Night Seven final** (Cardiff), 20 March 2025, against Michael van Gerwen.

"I had been playing very well but I must admit I hadn't picked up my darts since last Thursday," confessed Littler. "I had no idea that nine-darter was in, I just had to wait for Huw (Ware, referee) to call it."

– Luke Littler on his sixth professional nine-darter

DID YOU KNOW?

John Lowe was the first player to get a perfect score in a 501 game of darts on TV. During the 1984 World Matchplay Championship, Lowe hit the triple 20 six times in a row, followed by a triple 17, a triple 18 and finishing with a double 18.

RULES OF THE GAME

As a darts fan you may already know the rules of the game and how the dartboard works. For anyone reading this book who is new to the game, here's a brief overview to help you understand your doubles from your checkouts, and how the scoring works. You might not have been playing darts since you were 18 months old like Luke Littler, but once you've got your head around the rules and scoring system, your darts-playing journey can really begin!

There are several different versions of the game that can be played, but the most commonly played version is 501. This is the game played at all PDC events. There are also a number of different dartboards which are used around the world, but the standard board (pictured here) is the one used by the PDC and WDF in all their events.

STANDARD DARTBOARD STATS AND FACTS

Divided into 20 numbered sections, scoring 1 to 20 points

Diameter: 45.1 cm

Depth: 3.81 cm

Weight: 4.54–5.44 kg

Mounted height: with centre of the bullseye at 1.73 m from the floor

Diagonal distance from bullseye to the oche line: 2.93 m

Distance from the oche to the wall: 2.37 m

PDC official dartboard*: the Winmau Blade 6 Triple Core

(*Approved by the WDF, made from high-grade Kenyan sisal, a material made from agave plant fibres)

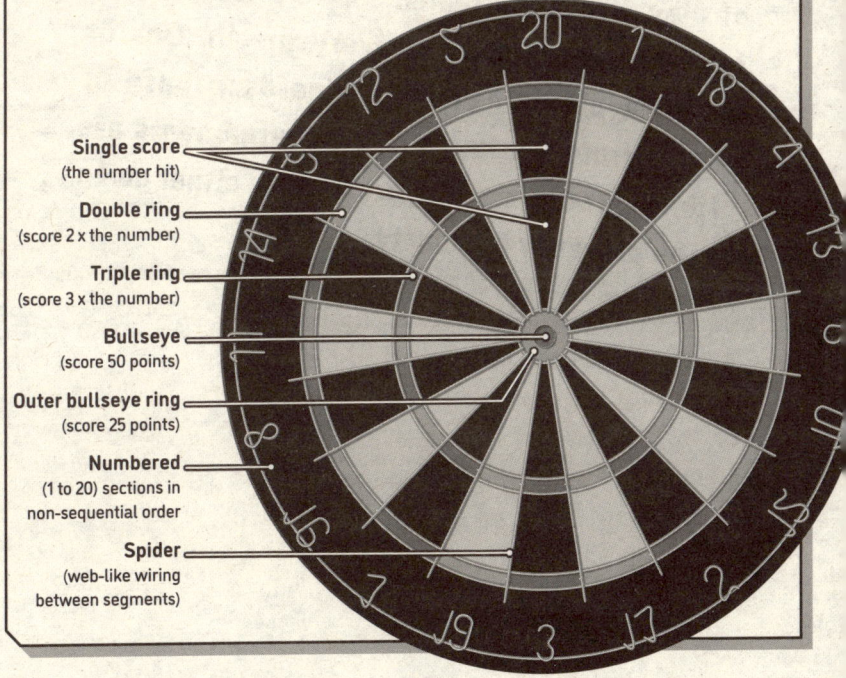

- **Single score** (the number hit)
- **Double ring** (score 2 x the number)
- **Triple ring** (score 3 x the number)
- **Bullseye** (score 50 points)
- **Outer bullseye ring** (score 25 points)
- **Numbered** (1 to 20) sections in non-sequential order
- **Spider** (web-like wiring between segments)

DID YOU KNOW?

A dartboard is used up to four times over the course of a tournament before being taken out of play. If the tournament is televised, then a new board is used for every match. Boards where a player has hit a nine-dart finish or boards from the finals of big tournaments are often signed by the players and are either given to the player or to charity.

MODERN LAYOUT

The layout of the modern board was created in 1896 by carpenter Brian Gamlin. Instead of numbering the segments in numerical order around the circle, where all the high numbers would be in a section together, he decided to mix up the higher and lower numbers. In this way, players who had previously just aimed for the high numbers hoping to hit any one of them would not be able to accidentally collect high scores. Some people dispute that Gamlin created the numbering system, saying that it was actually the wireworker Thomas William Buckle, who made dartboards for a living, who invented the standard system in 1913.

Each of the two players has three darts. To decide who plays first, each player throws a dart and the one who gets their dart nearest to the bullseye takes the first throw of the leg. They begin the first leg (game) of the match with 501 points. They must score down to zero by throwing their three darts on each turn.

Every score from a throw is deducted from 501. To win the leg, a player must be the first to bring their score to zero but they must end by throwing a double. So, for example, if a player has 40 points left, they need to hit a double 20 to win – hitting a single 20 twice will not win. If the points left don't divide exactly by two, then the player must throw a combination of scores with the last dart scoring a double. For example, if a player has 45 points left, they could hit a single 11 and a double 17; or a single 5 and a double 20 to win.

If a player scores more points than the number they have left, they can't take these points off their score, and they must wait until their next turn to try to finish again. This is known as 'busting' your score.

The total number of points scored on a player's final leg is called the 'checkout'.

To score double points, a player must hit the outer green and red coloured ring segments of the board. To score triple points they must hit the inner green and red coloured ring segments. Single points (of a value from 1 to 20) are scored by placing a dart in the black or white segments of the board.

For example, if a player hits the 20 outer-ring segment, they will score 20 x 2 = 40 points.

If they hit the white segment for 16, they will score 16 points.

If they hit the 15 inner-ring segment, they will score 15 x 3 = 45 points.

Hitting the red bullseye gives a player 50 points.

Hitting the green outer bullseye ring gives a player 25 points.

If a player misses any of the sections or misses the dartboard completely, or if their dart falls from the board, they don't score any points with that dart.

Players must stand behind the throwing line (oche) for their turn. In a standard game of darts, a player is required to throw all three darts on each of their turns unless they are finishing a leg to reach zero, which they can do in fewer throws.

> Calculating your scores and what throws you need to make during each leg requires nimble mental maths skills as well as the ability to think strategically. You might want to warm up your brain with some maths number challenges before your next game!

MATHS GENIUS?

Even though Luke says he was terrible at maths at school, he shows incredible mental maths abilities in his games, quickly navigating his way around the board to work out the next moves he needs to make to count down to zero.

"I was terrible at maths myself. But it's just the longer you practise, the quicker you get to know checkouts, scoring and finishing up and laying up your shots, and you know what to go for. So, the more you play, the more you get used to it."

– Luke Littler on his maths abilities in an interview with BBC Sport

> **DID YOU KNOW?**
> The 'oche' (pronounced like hockey without the h) was originally known as the 'hockey'. The word may originate from the old French word 'ocher' which means 'to cut a deep notch in'.

The number of legs required to win a match depends on the tournament being played. For example, in the PDC Premier League Championship, matches are played as the best of 11 legs, so the first player to get six legs is the winner. Some tournaments use sets as their scoring system. Each set is a specified number of legs. In the PDC World Darts Championship, a set is the best of five legs (the first player to win three legs wins), and the matches (depending on the round being played) are won on the best of 5, 7, 9, 11 or 13 predetermined sets. Luke Littler beat Michael van Gerwen 7–3 in the final match of the 2025 PDC World Darts Championship, in the best of 13 sets.

WORLD DARTS CHAMPIONSHIP MATCH SETS

First and second rounds: ..... best of 5 sets
Third and fourth rounds: ...... best of 7 sets
Quarter-finals: .... best of 9 sets
Semi-finals: .... best of 11 sets
Final: .... best of 13 sets

From the third round onwards, if a match goes to a final set, then that set must be won by two clear legs. If the score in this final set reaches five legs each, then a sudden-death leg must be played to determine the winner.

DID YOU KNOW?

As well as using the sets format for its tournament, the World Grand Prix uses a 'double in, double out' rule in its matches. This means the players must begin each game by hitting a double, as well as finishing their checkout on a double score.

CHOOSE YOUR ARROWS!

You may have heard darts players referring to their darts as 'arrows'. This is a throwback reference to an early form of darts that was played in medieval times. Soldiers played a game where they used the stubs of the arrows they had used in battle to throw at cut tree trunks or at the circular bottom of a wooden cask used as a target. The cracked sections created as the cask bottom dried out were the forerunners of the numbered sections on the modern dartboard.

Choosing the right darts can be confusing as there are many brands of varying lengths, as well as different weights and types of flights. Professional players have their favourites, and they are often the advertising 'face' and name of the brand they use.

Luke Littler uses Luke Littler Gen 1 Darts in 23 g from the darts brand Target. These darts were custom

OFFICIAL DARTS RULES
- Each dart must feature a barrel, a stem and a flight
- It must not exceed a maximum length of 200 mm
- It must not weigh more than 40 g

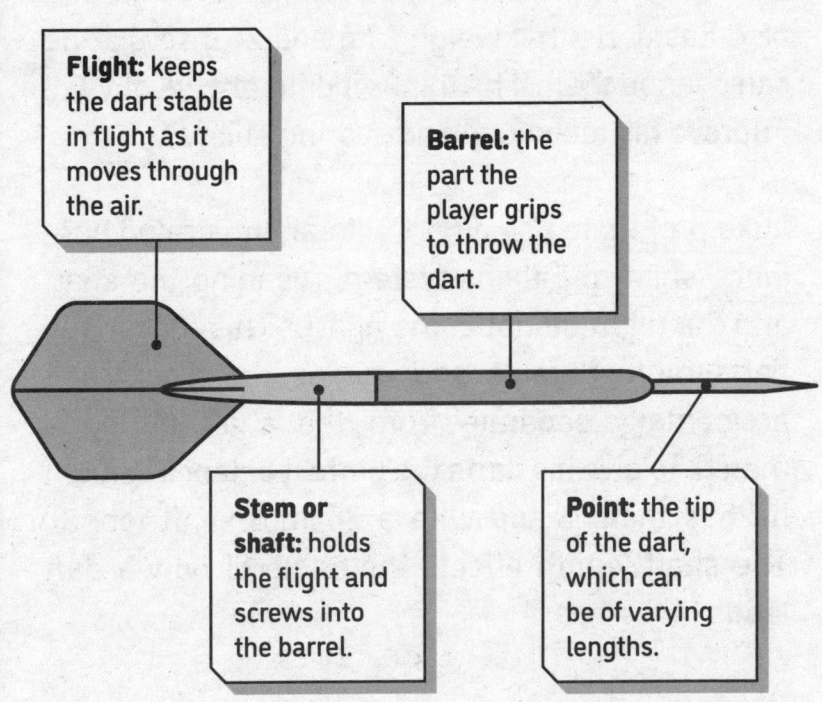

Flight: keeps the dart stable in flight as it moves through the air.

Barrel: the part the player grips to throw the dart.

Stem or shaft: holds the flight and screws into the barrel.

Point: the tip of the dart, which can be of varying lengths.

designed by Target in collaboration with Luke after he became the JDC Youth World Champion in 2023 to meet his exact requirements and help him maximize his performance.

Sometimes a player will change the weight of their darts during a tournament to improve their game. As well as his preferred match weight of 23 g, Luke also has darts that weigh 22 g and 24 g so that he can change them if he thinks a different weight will improve his technique and scoring ability.

Luke prefers to use a dart with an integrated one-piece shaft and flight system, meaning the shaft and the flight do not come apart.* This makes the darts more durable and means the flight can't accidentally separate from the shaft during a match. To give his darts the perfect balance in flight he has them made with a 26 mm shaft length. The shaft length effects the angle of how a dart lands in the board.

*Some darts are made with the shaft and flight as one piece and some come in segments.

Luke's darts are made of 90% tungsten, a heavy and dense material, which means he can have the barrels made very thin without losing any of the weight he prefers. Luke prefers to have a thinner barrel to hold, but he still needs it to have a certain weight to give the dart lift during flight. The tungsten material has the required weight but can be moulded into a thinner shape. Along with a longer point, this means more darts can fit in a smaller segment on the dartboard.

Look out for Target's 'Loadout' darts set, which Luke worked on. These darts are more affordable. They have grooves on the shaft for better finger grip and they are decorated with splashes of Luke's signature colours: purple and yellow.

DID YOU KNOW?

Luke Littler prefers a longer point of 45 mm on his darts. A longer point covers less of the target on the board which allows a player to fit one or two more darts in the same segment, giving them a better chance of hitting higher scores in the double, triple and bullseye segments.

THROWING SKILLS AND TECHNIQUES

Like any sport, the more you practise, the better and more skilled you become. It's the same in darts. Top players practise for many hours to perfect their techniques, experimenting with how they grip their darts and with the pace and action of their throw.

Consistent practice improves your stamina, focus and mental strength under pressure. It also develops your muscle memory – your body remembers your technique without you having to consciously think about it, and this improves your shot accuracy.

LUKE'S TECHNIQUE

Luke locks his eyes on his target while bringing his dart back towards him. He releases it with a smooth flick of his wrist from a low elbow throw, and then extends his arm after the dart leaves his hand.

Luke holds his darts in a four-finger grip, using his thumb, index, middle and ring fingers. Your grip style is important as this gives you control over the dart's flight trajectory to the board. It might take some time to find a grip that works for you. Luke puts his index finger and thumb on the back of the barrel and the front of the shaft. His middle finger sits on the front of the barrel and the point of the dart lies on his ring finger.

Every player finds their own throwing and grip technique. You might have already established yours, but if you are still experimenting, go online and watch videos of Luke and other darts players to see how they do it. Remember to always ask a grown-up's permission before using the internet.

LITTLERMANIA

As the youngest world champion in darts history, Luke Littler is continuing to make his mark on the professional darting world stage. His rapid rise to fame, dubbed 'Littlermania' on social media, has led to an increased interest in the sport, especially among young people, inspiring many of them to take up darts themselves. More and more darts academies are popping up in the UK as the demand for the sport increases.

Luke has taken the internet by storm and has thousands of fans. He already has more Instagram followers than any other darts player, retired or currently playing, and he has been made into memes. The video of 18-month-old Luke throwing toy darts at a magnetic board was a viral sensation. In 2024, 'The Nuke' was the most searched-for athlete! And to top this off, his World Darts Championship final in January 2025 became the most viewed non-football event the Sky Sports channel has shown.

With worldwide fame comes lots of money in earnings from match winnings and sponsorship deals with companies like National Rail, Xbox, Boohoo Man and KP Nuts. Luke has even got his own range of purple and yellow darts with Target Darts.

However, none of this would have been possible without hard work and dedication. Luke may have stepped into the limelight seemingly overnight, but he has put in hours of practice to perfect his talent. His competition match schedule is exhausting. If Luke isn't playing in a match, he is practising for one to keep up his skills and improve his techniques. He hopes to inspire the next generation of darts players and to keep winning titles.

Luke continues to live at home with his parents, and even though his earnings from darts tournament winnings, sponsorships and merchandise now exceed £1 million, Luke gets a monthly allowance to maintain a sense of normality in his life. He doesn't go out splashing money around and buying expensive items. Like other lads and lasses his own age, Luke likes to occasionally treat himself, buying new clothes – like Under Armour tracksuits, one of his favourite brands – and FIFA points for his Xbox. And despite being famous around the world, Luke still makes time to visit his local darts academy, St Helens, where his own darts dream journey started, to chat with other aspiring young players.

DOWN TIME

When Luke isn't practising darts or competing in darts tournaments, he likes to play video games. He is a big fan of EA Sports FC and enjoys playing the Pro Clubs feature where individual players control one player on a team. Sometimes he live-streams his games.

DID YOU KNOW?

Luke's favourite takeaway in his hometown is called Hot Spot. It now has a wrap named after him! How awesome is that?

THE OTHER 'BEAUTIFUL GAME'

Shortly after his World Darts Championship debut in 2024, where he lost to Luke Humphries, Luke got to meet Sir Alex Ferguson, former manager of Manchester United football team and one of Luke's childhood idols, at the Old Trafford football stadium in Manchester. This was a huge moment for Luke. He has supported Manchester United since 2013, when Ferguson was still the manager.

If you haven't already, find out if there are any youth darts academies or clubs in your local area that you could join to start playing the sport on a regular basis. This is a great way to meet other people that love darts as much as you do, and to start playing in amateur tournaments and youth competitions. Who knows? You could be the next Luke Littler.

FROM TODDLER TO WORLD CHAMPION

Luke's dad, an amateur darts player himself, bought his 18-month-old son a magnetic dartboard. The toddler instantly took to the game and showed good follow-through on his throw. Little did Luke's parents know then that this simple gift would set their son up for his future meteoric career as a professional darts player.

By the age of four, Luke was playing on a proper dartboard, going on to score his first perfect 180 at the age of six. By the time Luke was eight, realizing that their son was showing a talent for the game, Luke's parents started taking their son to their local pubs (where dart boards could often be found), four or five times a week, so he could practise.

Soon after this, Luke joined his local darts academy,

St Helens. The coaches there saw Luke's potential, and aged just 10, he began playing in under-21 leagues in Junior Darts Corporation (JDC) events.

Luke was a natural. He was also very driven to win. He loved playing and the more matches he won, the more determined he was to work hard to get to the next level.

In 2019, Luke won the WDF England Youth Grand Prix. By 13 years old he had scored his first perfect nine-dart leg finish. That same year, he won the 2020 Isle of Man Masters Youth competition, before Covid stopped all competitive play.

During this time, Luke's exceptional darts achievements started getting noticed by people in the world of the sport. Target Darts, a specialist supplier of an extensive range of darts products, and a company who sponsor some of the world's leading darts players, liked what they were seeing. They signed Luke up for their Elite 1 mentoring programme to help him develop his skills to become a professional darts player.

Luke's darting prowess was beginning to really take off. In 2021, aged 14, he won the WDF England Open Youth title, followed by his first seniors title at the Irish Open, where he beat Barry Copeland 6–2 in legs. This was a pivotal moment because it meant he qualified for the 2022 WDF World Darts Championship, one of the top tournaments in the sport. In November, he hit a nine-darter at the Junior Darts Corporation (JDC) Michael van Gerwen Masters tournament, finishing his year on a high.

2022 was another great year for Luke, one in which he achieved several record-breaking feats. In January, he won the JDC Super 16, beating Eleanor Cairns in the final. In March, he reached the finals of the WDF Isle of Man Classic competition, after winning the youth Isle of Man Open competition.

Although Luke didn't win the 2022 WDF World Darts Championship, he was now a seeded player, meaning he was recognized as a top player. In June, he won the Romanian Classic and then won the gold medal in three men's competitions (team, singles and overall) at the 2022 WDF Europe Cup Youth.

> **DID YOU KNOW?**
> Seeding in sport is the practice of separating the most skilled players from each other in the early rounds of a competition. This is done so that the best players don't knock each other out early in a tournament. They get to play each other later in the competition, pitting their skills against each other.

On the back of these wins, Luke was selected to play in the 2022 WDF Europe Cup, where he was part of the team that won a gold medal.

At the end of 2022, Luke won the JDC World Darts Championship, beating Harry Gregory 5–0 in legs.

2023 saw Luke's star continuing to rise. In one weekend, he won both the WDF British Classic competition and the British Open. He went on to win the third and fourth seasons of the MODUS Super Series (a weekly competition for top international players), and made his debut at a major PDC event, the 2023 UK Open. There, he reached the fourth round.

As if this wasn't enough, Luke won five titles in the 2023 PDC Development Tour series. He finished second, losing the final to Gian van Veen, in the 2023 Development Tour Order of Merit. Although he hadn't come first, Luke's second position meant he qualified to play in the 2024 PDC World Darts Championship, one of the top tournaments in the world of darts.

Gian van Veen's victory over Luke was short-lived. In November, Luke beat him 6–4 in the 2023 PDC World Youth Championship. In December, Luke was also victorious in the JDC World Darts Championship, defeating Álmos Kovács 5–3.

The world was starting to talk about Luke Littler. The 16-year-old's concentration and his precision and strategic thinking in his gameplay was incredible. He was focused, driven and remained calm under pressure – impressive attributes in any player, but especially so in such a young person.

The end of 2023 and start of 2024 saw Luke's first appearance in the 2024 PDC World Darts Championship. Thrown into the spotlight, with the world watching, he coolly beat Christian Kist 3–0 in the first round. In his second round he beat Andrew Gilding 3–1. Keeping his nerve, Luke then went on to beat Matt Campbell 4–1 in the third round. In the fourth round, up against Raymond Van Barneveld, the five-time world champion, Luke defeated his childhood hero 4–1.

Moving into the quarterfinals he defeated Brendan Dolan 5–1. In the semi-final, up against Rob Cross, another one of his darts heroes, Luke won the match 6-2.

Luke lost the final to Luke Humphries 7–4. Initially, Humphries fell behind 4–2, but then he made a spectacular comeback, winning five successive sets to claim the title.

Undeterred, and now riding on a wave of well-deserved recognition, Luke soared through 2024, breaking records and winning 10 titles. That year he won 145 of the 189 games he played. He achieved international victories at the Bahrain Darts Masters and the Poland Darts Masters. Nearer to home, Luke defeated Luke Humphries in the final of the Premier League Darts tournament and won the Grand Slam of Darts, securing his place at the top of the darts world as one of the sport's shining new talents.

DID YOU KNOW?

Luke Littler's journey to the big darts leagues started in the youth leagues. These leagues are an excellent place for young players to hone their techniques and skills in a fun and less pressurized environment, and where they can learn good sportsmanship and gain confidence. The PDC introduced its World Youth Championships for players of 16 to 23 years old in 2011. The winner of the first tournament was Arron Monk. He defeated Michael van Gerwen 6–4 in the final. Luke took the title in 2023, beating Gian van Veen with the same score. Gian van Veen went on to win the title the following year.

AT A GLANCE: LUKE'S SENSATIONAL 2024!

- **10 TOURNAMENTS WON**
- **PDC RANKING 4TH**
- **FOUR NINE-DART FINISHES**
- **WIN PERCENTAGE 77%**
- **CHECKOUT RATE 41.35%***
- **YEARLY AVERAGE 99.26****

* A player must hit a double or the bullseye to finish a leg. The checkout rate is the ratio of successful double finishes to the total number of attempts at a double. A high checkout percentage shows how skilled a player is at hitting doubles.

** The three-dart average is the average of the total score achieved with each turn of three darts in a game of 501. The yearly average refers to a player's three-dart average calculated across all the matches they have played in a calendar year. A strong yearly average for a professional player is in the high 90s or over 100. A tournament average is a player's three-dart average over all the matches played in that tournament.

LITTLER'S 2024 WINNER'S RECORD

BAHRAIN DARTS MASTERS:
8–5 against Michael van Gerwen

PLAYERS CHAMPIONSHIP 1:
8–7 against Ryan Searle

BELGIAN DARTS OPEN:
8–7 against Rob Cross

AUSTRIAN DARTS OPEN:
8–4 against Joe Cullen

PREMIER LEAGUE:
11–7 against Luke Humphries

POLAND DARTS MASTERS:
8–3 against Rob Cross

PLAYERS CHAMPIONSHIP 15:
8–6 against Wessel Nijman

WORLD SERIES OF DARTS FINALS:
11–4 against Michael Smith

PLAYERS CHAMPIONSHIP 20:
8–7 against Stephen Bunting

GRAND SLAM OF DARTS:
16–3 against Martin Lukeman

BAHRAIN DARTS MASTERS
- First World Series of Darts win.
- First televised nine-dart finish against Nathan Aspinall.

PLAYERS CHAMPIONSHIPS
- Debut in the PDC Players Championship.
- Second nine-dart finish against Michele Turetta.

BELGIAN DARTS OPEN
- First European Tour event.
- Third nine-dart finish against Rob Cross in the final.

AUSTRIAN DARTS OPEN
- Beat top players like Damon Heta and Ross Smith to make it into the final against Joe Cullen.

PREMIER LEAGUE DARTS
- Debut in this tournament and first Premier League of Darts title.
- Fourth nine-dart finish against Luke Humphries.
- Defeated 2023 and 2024 world champions Michael Smith and Luke Humphries.

POLAND DARTS MASTERS
- Defeated former world champion Michael Smith in the semi-final and his childhood hero, good friend and darting rival, Rob Cross once again in another final.

WORLD SERIES OF DARTS FINALS
- Defeated five-time champion Michael van Gerwen in the semi-finals, went on to defeat former world champion Michael Smith in the final.

GRAND SLAM OF DARTS
- Achieved a tournament average of 104.99, the third highest ever in the tournament's history.
- His win earned Littler fifth place on the PDC Order of Merit, an incredible achievement, not only for such a young player, but also considering Littler had only begun his professional career at the beginning of that year.

HITTING THE BULLSEYE!

At the top of his game, ranking as the number four seed, Luke was excited to play in the 2025 PDC World Darts Championship. This was his chance to try to win the top darts sporting trophy. Triumphing in each round and living up to his darts name 'The Nuke', Luke took the tournament by storm. His playing was electric, and he stunned the crowds and his opponents with his calm demeanour and precision techniques.

This was his moment. Stepping up to the oche for the final match, Luke crushed the three-time world champion Michael van Gerwen 7–3 to take home the trophy. On 3 January 2025, aged 17, just a few weeks before his 18th birthday, Luke Littler became the youngest person ever to win the PDC World Darts Championship.

2025 PDC WORLD DARTS CHAMPIONSHIP

(15 December 2024 to 3 January 2025)

THE ROUNDS

The tournament consists of four rounds followed by the quarter finals, semi-finals and the final.

In round one, 64 players compete against each other for places in round two. Only 32 players will progress.

The 32 winners of round one play the 32 highest ranked seeded players, who have gone straight into round two.

The 32 winners of round two compete against each other in round three for 16 places in round four.

The 16 winners of round three play for 8 places in the quarter finals.

The 4 winners of the quarter finals play in the semi-finals for a place in the final.

GAME PLAY

The matches are played in set format. A player must win a minimum of three sets to win the match. To win a set, a player must win three legs. Players must score 501 points and finish on a double to win a leg.

In rounds one and two, matches are played to the best of five sets.

In rounds three and four, matches are played to the best of seven sets.

In the quarter finals, matches are played to the best of nine sets.

In the semi-finals, matches are played to the best of 11 sets.

In the final, the match is played to the best of 13 sets, the winner being the first player to win seven sets.

THE PLAYERS

There are 96 players competing to win the title. Those players consist of:

- The 32 highest ranked players on the PDC Order of Merit. They are seeded and go straight into the second round.

- The top 32 not yet qualified players from the 2024 PDC Pro Tour Order of Merit. They are entered in round one.

- The 32 international qualifiers. They are also entered in the first round.

TOP 5 SEEDED DARTS PLAYERS IN PDC WORLD DARTS CHAMPIONSHIP 2025

1 Luke Humphries
   – knocked out in the fourth round
2 Michael Smith
   – knocked out in the second round
3 Michael van Gerwen
   – beaten in the final
4 Luke Littler
   – the winner
5 Rob Cross
   – knocked out in the second round

LUKE LITTLER'S MATCHES

Round 2: Luke Littler 3–1 Ryan Meikle
Round 3: Luke Littler 4–1 Ian White
Round 4: Luke Littler 4–3 Ryan Joyce
Quarter final: Luke Littler 5–2 Nathan Aspinall
Semi-final: Luke Littler 6–1 Stephen Bunting
Final: Luke Littler 7–3 Michael van Gerwen

QUARTER FINALS
Chris Dobey 5–3 Gerwyn Price
 Set 1: 2–3; Set 2: 1–3; Set 3: 3–1; Set 4: 3–2;
 Set 5: 3–2; Set 6: 3–0; Set 7: 2–3; Set 8: 3–1

Michael van Gerwen 5–3 Callan Rydz
 Set 1: 3–2; Set 2: 0–3; Set 3: 3–2; Set 4: 1–3;
 Set 5: 3–2; Set 6: 3–1; Set 7: 1–3; Set 8: 3–2

Stephen Bunting 5–2 Peter Wright
 Set 1: 3–1; Set 2: 3–1; Set 3: 3–2; Set 4: 3–0;
 Set 5: 0–3; Set 6: 1–3; Set 7: 3–0

Luke Littler 5–2 Nathan Aspinall
 Set 1: 3–0; Set 2: 3–1; Set 3: 2–3; Set 4: 3–2;
 Set 5: 3–1; Set 6: 2–3; Set 7: 3–0

SEMI-FINALS
Michael van Gerwen 6–1 Chris Dobey
 Set 1: 3–1; Set 2: 3–2; Set 3: 0–3; Set 4: 3–0;
 Set 5: 3–1; Set 6: 3–2; Set 7: 3–1

Luke Littler 6–1 Stephen Bunting
 Set 1: 3–2; Set 2: 3–1; Set 3: 3–2; Set 4: 3–1;
 Set 5: 1–3; Set 6: 3–2; Set 7: 3–1

FINAL

Luke Littler 7–3 Michael van Gerwen
Set 1: 3–1; Set 2: 3–0; Set 3: 3–1; Set 4: 3–1; Set 5: 1–3;
Set 6: 3–2; Set 7: 2–3; Set 8: 3–0; Set 9: 1–3; Set 10: 3–0

PRIZE MONEY (2025)

Winner: £500,000

Runner-up: £200,000

Semi-finalists (2 players): £100,000

Quarter-finalists (4 players): £50,000

Fourth round losers *(8 players):* £35,000

Third round losers (16 players): £25,000

Second round losers (32 players): £15,000

First round losers (32 players): £7,500

Nine-dart finish (to each player that hits one):
£60,000 bonus

SID WADDELL TROPHY

This prestigious PDC World Darts Championship trophy is named after the legendary commentator Sid Waddell, who was the voice of the sport on the BBC for nearly two decades, and then on Sky Sports for nearly two decades more. Sadly, Sid passed away in August 2012 after battling cancer. In 2021, the PDC renamed the trophy in his honour. Sid's last commentary for the sport was at the Premier League final in 2012 between Phil Taylor and Simon Whitlock. Taylor won the title 10–7. This was his sixth and final Premier League victory. Both finalists hit nine-dart finishes during the tournament. You can bet Sid had a lot to say about these two champions!

DID YOU KNOW?

Luke Littler was seeded fourth in the PDC World Darts Championship so he didn't have to compete in the first round. Luke Humphries, seeded number one, was the defending champion, having defeated Luke Littler 7–4 in the 2024 PDC final.

DID YOU KNOW?
Luke made his debut at the PDC World Darts Championship in 2024 to the excited crowds chanting, "You've got school in the morning!"

DID YOU KNOW?
Dutch international qualifier Christian Kist and the ninth seeded Australian player Damon Heta were the only two players in the 2025 PDC World Dart's Championship to hit nine-darters. Kist lost his match in round one, 3–1, to Madars Razma who went out in the third round. Heta made it through to round three, where he lost 3–4 to Luke Woodhouse, who went out in the fourth round.

DID YOU KNOW?

In 2024, Luke was named BBC Young Sports Personality of the Year, the first darts player ever to win this award. He was also the runner-up for BBC Sports Personality of the Year, behind the winner, middle-distance runner Keely Hodgkinson.

DID YOU KNOW?

When Luke Littler became the youngest world champion in PDC history, he beat the record previously held by Michael van Gerwen, who was 24 years old when he won the tournament in 2014.

RECORD BREAKER!

★ Luke was the youngest player ever to win a match both in the WDF World Darts Championship (2022) and the PDC World Darts Championship (2024).

★ Aged 16, a month before his 17th birthday, Luke became the youngest-ever finalist in the 2024 PDC World Darts Championship. Scoring an average of 106.12, he achieved the highest-ever recorded score for a newcomer in the tournament's history.

☆ At the 2024 Bahrain Darts Masters Luke became the youngest player to hit a televised nine-darter, two days before his 17th birthday.

☆ In 2024, Luke hit a record-breaking number of 180s – 836 in total – the highest number of any professional player that year.

☆ In 2025, a few days before his 18th birthday, Luke became the youngest person ever to win the PDC World Darts Championship.

Previous winners and runners-up of the PDC World Darts Championship since its first tournament

Year	Winner	Sets		Sets	Runner-up
2025	Luke Littler	7	–	3	Michael van Gerwen
2024	Luke Humphries	7	–	4	Luke Littler
2023	Michael Smith	7	–	4	Michael van Gerwen
2022	Peter Wright	7	–	5	Michael Smith
2021	Gerwyn Price	7	–	3	Gary Anderson
2020	Peter Wright	7	–	3	Michael van Gerwen
2019	Michael van Gerwen	7	–	3	Michael Smith
2018	Rob Cross	7	–	2	Phil Taylor
2017	Michael van Gerwen	7	–	3	Gary Anderson
2016	Gary Anderson	7	–	5	Adrian Lewis
2015	Gary Anderson	7	–	6	Phil Taylor
2014	Michael van Gerwen	7	–	4	Peter Wright
2013	Phil Taylor	7	–	4	Michael van Gerwen
2012	Adrian Lewis	7	–	3	Andy Hamilton
2011	Adrian Lewis	7	–	5	Gary Anderson
2010	Phil Taylor	7	–	3	Simon Whitlock

Year	Winner	Sets		Sets	Runner-up
2009	Phil Taylor	7	–	1	Raymond van Barneveld
2008	John Part	7	–	2	Kirk Shepherd
2007	Raymond van Barneveld	7	–	6	Phil Taylor
2006	Phil Taylor	7	–	0	Peter Manley
2005	Phil Taylor	7	–	4	Mark Dudbridge
2004	Phil Taylor	7	–	6	Kevin Painter
2003	John Part	7	–	6	Phil Taylor
2002	Phil Taylor	7	–	0	Peter Manley
2001	Phil Taylor	7	–	0	John Part
2000	Phil Taylor	7	–	3	Dennis Priestley
1999	Phil Taylor	6	–	2	Peter Manley
1998	Phil Taylor	6	–	0	Dennis Priestley
1997	Phil Taylor	6	–	3	Dennis Priestley
1996	Phil Taylor	6	–	4	Dennis Priestley
1995	Phil Taylor	6	–	2	Rod Harrington
1994	Dennis Priestley	6	–	1	Phil Taylor

THE WORLD OF DARTS

Darts is often tarred with the image of being a hobbyist pub game, played by older men drinking pints of beer. And although darts is a popular pub and club game, played by all ages and genders, it has become a worldclass professional sport, with highly skilled elite players from all walks of life. Darts was officially granted sports status in the UK in 2005 by Sports England.

More and more young players are coming up through the ranks at every level, from playing in youth academies to qualifying for the top professional tournaments and leagues, where they are matching the skills of the established, well-known darting heroes. Young stars like Luke Littler have got the world talking positively about darts, a sport that requires not only physical skills and techniques but also mathematical tactics, precision, strategic thinking, unwavering concentration and the ability to remain calm under pressure.

If you are reading this book, you are probably already a fan of the sport, or maybe even a youth player yourself, and you might be discovering that there are many leagues and tournaments, from youth to professional, that are played around the world on an annual circuit. If you don't yet know your BDOs from your PDCs or WDCs and WDFs, here's a brief overview to get you up to speed.

> **British Darts Organisation (BDO):** the sport's governing body in the UK, established in 1973.
>
> **UK Darts Association (UKDA):** the new name of the BDO since 2020.
>
> **World Darts Federation (WDF):** the global body for amateur darts, established in 1976. In 2020, when the BDO closed and became the UKDA, the WDF took over the control of all its events,

including its World Championship, normally held at the Lakeside venue in Surrey, England.

World Darts Council (WDC): an independent governing body, established in 1992 after the split from the BDO. Not recognized by the BDO until 1997.

Profession Darts Corporation (PDC): the former WDC. Changed its name to PDC in 1997 when the BDO recognized its right to exist independently. Has its own world rankings.

SPLITTING THE ARROW

Darts was first televised on British television in 1937. Over the next few decades, the popularity of the sport grew, with more viewers tuning in to watch the televised matches and fans turning up in large numbers to watch live games.

During the 1970s and 1980s, televised darts hit an all-time high, but by the end of the 1980s, TV channels started dropping the matches as the image of the sport became negative. TV bosses wanted to attract younger and more affluent viewers. The game of darts was associated with older, lower income audiences, beer drinking players and badly behaved fans.

By 1989, the BDO Embassy World Championship at the Lakeside was the only televised darts event. This was not good for the top professional players, who relied on the televised matches for their livelihoods.

Eventually, this led to a dispute in 1992 between a group of top professional darts players, who wanted more coverage of their matches and better prize money, and the sport's governing body, the British Darts Organisation (BDO). From the BDO's first event in 1978 up until 1993, there had only been one unified professional World Darts Championship. In 1993, there was a split.

WORLD DARTS COUNCIL (WDC)

In January 1992, the top 16 players in the world got together to form their own group, the World Darts Council (WDC). In 1993, when the BDO refused to recognize the WDC as a separate body, the WDC said they would boycott the next World Championship.

In response, the BDO banned the WDC, which included every world champion up until that point, from all BDO sponsored events. Shortly afterwards, the WDF also banned the WDC rebels from all their events.

In 1993, on Boxing Day, the WDC held their own world championship. The final on the 2 January 1994 was won by top worldclass player Denis Priestly. He defeated Phil Taylor 6-1. The BDO held their usual Embassy World Championship later in January 1994, minus all the star players that had left to form the WDC.

Professional Darts Corporation (PDC)

Finally in 1997, after a lengthy court dispute between the BDO and the WDC, the BDO recognized that all players should be able to choose which darts events and competitions they played in, whether they were BDO sponsored or WDC.

The WDC dropped its claim to be an independent world governing body and renamed itself the Professional Darts Corporation (PDC). The PDC recognized the BDO as the governing body for darts in the UK and the WDF as the sport's governing body worldwide.

As part of the agreement all parties agreed that the top 16 players, plus any UK home country players ranked between 17 and 32, in each year's BDO World Championship and the top 16 players in each year's PDC World Darts Championship could not enter the other competition in the following year.

This ruling has meant that many professional darts players choose to switch to PDC events once they qualify, as the PDC is recognized as the leading professional darts organization and has a more dominant presence in professional darts worldwide.

DID YOU KNOW?

In 2023, Luke Littler had to choose whether to compete in the WDF World Championship at the Lakeside or to compete in the more prestigious PDC World Darts Championship at Alexandra Palace in London. He chose the PDC tournament, which it turned out was his ticket to the top! Luke now competes in PDC events worldwide as a professional darts player.

World Darts Federation (WDF)

The WDF, the recognized governing body for amateur darts globally, is made up of a group of darts federations that together promote the sport and organize international tournaments and darts events around the world, including the World Cup and the World Masters.

The federation is non-political and non-profitmaking and works to maintain the highest standards in the sport worldwide. Unlike the PDC events, the WDF tournaments don't have as much live TV coverage. Shortened screenings of the World Masters and the World Championships are aired.

"I want to say a massive thank you to the WDF for the opportunities I've had to play around Europe and on the Lakeside stage in the 2022 World Championships. I think the experience I've gained through playing in and winning tournaments with literally hundreds of entries will set me up nicely for my career in darts. It is sad that I won't be able to take up the challenge of playing in the WDF Lakeside World Championships, but I wish all of the players and the WDF team every success at Lakeside and in the future."

– Luke Littler choosing the PDC World Darts Championship over the WDF World Championship

MAIN WDF EVENTS

- **WORLD CHAMPIONSHIP** (annual)
- **WORLD MASTERS** (annual)
- **WORLD CUP** (international, every two years, singles, pairs and team events)
- **EUROPE CUP** (international, every two years, singles, pairs and team events)
- **ASIA-PACIFIC CUP** (international, every two years, singles, pairs and team events)
- **AMERICAS CUP** (international, every two years, singles, pairs and team events)
- **INTERNATIONAL OPENS**
- **NATIONAL AND REGIONAL EVENTS**

MAIN PDC EVENTS

- **WORLD DARTS CHAMPIONSHIP**
  (annual)*

- **PREMIER LEAGUE DARTS**
  (annual, runs between February and May as a weekly league)*

- **WORLD MATCHPLAY** (annual)*

- **GRAND SLAM OF DARTS** (annual – allows players from WDF to also play)

- **UK OPEN** (annual)

- **EUROPEAN CHAMPIONSHIP**
  (Pro Tour – annual event open to top 32 players on the Players Championship Order of Merit)

*part of the 'Triple Crown' – the three biggest and most prestigious darts tournaments.

- **PLAYERS CHAMPIONSHIPS FINALS** (annual – at the end of 30 events held across the calendar year, the top 64 players take part in the Finals)

- **WORLD GRAND PRIX** (annual)

- **WORLD WINMAU MASTERS** (annual)

- **WORLD CUP OF DARTS** (annual)

- **EUROPEAN TOUR** (Pro Tour – series of events held annually across Europe)

- **CHALLENGE TOUR** (annual events for players who played in the PDC Qualifying School but who didn't win a PDC Tour Card)

- **DEVELOPMENT TOUR ORDER OF MERIT** (offers young players, aged 16–23, a chance to compete in PDC events, followed by the PDC Winmau World Youth Championship. Top two players earn a PDC Tour Card and a place in the World Darts Championship)

- **WOMEN'S SERIES**

PDC WOMEN'S SERIES

PDC's World Darts Championship, the ProTour, Challenge Tour and Development Tour are open to all players. The PDC Women's Series (introduced in 2020) and the Women's World Matchplay (introduced in 2022) are for female players only. They were introduced to give women players the opportunity to compete in PDC events.

The WDF holds a separate World Championship for women (introduced in 2001), whereas the PDC doesn't. Some women players aren't happy about this and feel that the PDC should introduce their own Women's World Championship.

From 2025, top players from the PDC Women's Series get the chance to qualify for the PDC World Masters and the Grand Slam of Darts. They are also offered free entry for a place at the PDC Qualifying School. However, if they compete in the WDF

Women's World Championship they can't compete in the PDC World Darts Championship in the same year because of the 1997 rule made after the BDO and WDC split in 1992.

There are 24 tournaments in the Women's Series circuit, with a £2,000 prize for the winner of each tournament. Like many sports, women darts players are not paid as much as their male counterparts.

DID YOU KNOW?
Fallon Sherrock was the first woman in PDC history to hit a nine-dart finish. She achieved this feat at the PDC Challenge Tour, Event Nine, in her match against Marco Verhofstad, defeating him 5–3. Fallon also made history in the 2020 PDC World Darts Championship when she became the first female player to win a match at this event.

PDC TOUR CARD

You may have heard sport commentators talking about a player's PDC Tour Card. This card is like a golden ticket into the world of professional darts.

Every year, the PDC grants a Tour Card to 128 darts players, with the top 64 ranked players in the PDC Order of Merit automatically receiving one-year cards. A Tour Card allows players to compete in the PDC Pro Tour tournaments – Players Championships, European Tours and UK Open. It is like an exclusive membership card into the top level of professional darts.

Players can earn a two-year Tour Card by competing in the Qualifying School, and the top two players from the PDC Challenge Tour and the PDC Development Tour automatically receive a two-year Tour Card.

Once a player's card is no longer valid, or they lose it due to poor performance, they have to compete in the Qualifying School event. There are only a limited number of Tour Cards up for grabs in this event.

The system is designed to ensure that only the best players get to compete at the highest level. Having a Tour Card adds a competitive edge to every professional tournament, as players could potentially lose their card if they don't perform well in their matches across the annual circuit. It does also put a lot of pressure on the players – they need to stay at the top of their performance to retain their professional status.

LUKE'S TOUR CARD

Luke Littler gained his Tour Card for the start of the 2024 circuit, the year that saw the schoolboy from Warrington go from promising young player, fresh off his Youth Championship title, to phenomenal rising star reaching the final of the PDC World Darts Championship, followed by ten big tournament wins throughout the year.

"It's been unbelievable. Like I've said, I just wanted to win one game, come back after Christmas, and that was it. That's the only goal I set. So, this is just a massive, massive bonus."

– Luke Littler on getting a place in the quarter-finals of his debut PDC World Darts Championship in 2024

ORDER OF MERIT

Another term thrown around in the world of darts is the Order of Merit, which is a ranking system. There are eight main Order of Merit rankings, and like the Tour Card, these orders grant ranked status and allow players to qualify for the top professional tournaments. Check out the list below to learn about the different Merits.

1. PDC ORDER OF MERIT

This is the most prestigious ranking in darts. The list is based on the prize money players earn at PDC events over a two-year period. It determines who qualifies for the major PDC tournaments. The top 32 in the list automatically qualify for the second round at the PDC World Darts Championship. The top 16 players automatically qualify for the World Matchplay, World Grand Prix and Euro Tour tournaments.

2. PDC PRO TOUR ORDER OF MERIT

Money that is earned in the Players Championship tournaments and also the European Tour counts towards this Order of Merit. It gives players who haven't directly qualified for major tournaments through the PDC Order of Merit a chance to take part in major events. The top 32 players will receive an invitation to the PDC World Darts Championship. The top 16 players on the list will qualify for tournaments such as World Matchplay, World Grand Prix and Euro Tour tournaments.

3. EUROPEAN TOUR ORDER OF MERIT

This merit is based on players' performances in European Tour tournaments. It is the only way a player can qualify for the European Championships. The top 32 players on the list will be invited to play.

4. PLAYERS CHAMPIONSHIP ORDER OF MERIT

A ranking list based on prize money won in Players Championship events during a calendar year. The 64 players who win the most prize money qualify for this Order of Merit and can play in the Players Championship Finals.

5. WORLD SERIES ORDER OF MERIT

This list is based on a player's performance in the World Series of Darts tournaments, which are played around the world. A player's seeding is based on their position on the list. The top player automatically qualifies for the World Series Finals.

6. CHALLENGE TOUR ORDER OF MERIT

This merit offers the top players who took part in the Qualifying School event, but did not earn a Tour Card, a chance to enter the Players Championship tournaments as alternates. The top two players can compete in the PDC World Darts Championship, and they will receive a PDC Tour Card for the following two calendar seasons. The top player receives an invitation to compete in the Grand Slam of Darts. The top eight players are given entry to the following year's UK Open.

7. DEVELOPMENT TOUR OF ORDER OF MERIT

This merit is for young talented players between the ages of 16 and 23. Players are ranked based on how much prize money they earn in the PDC Development Tour tournaments.

In 2025, a new ruling was brought in that states that players in the top 64 of the PDC Order of Merit will no longer be allowed to compete in Development Tour tournaments, but they will still have access to the World Youth Championship.

The top eight players of this ranked group will be able to gain entry to the following year's UK Open tournament. The top two players may compete in the PDC World Darts Championship and will receive a PDC Tour Card for the following two seasons. The number one player on this merit list will receive an invitation to the Grand Slam of Darts.

8. WOMEN'S SERIES ORDER OF MERIT

This merit is specifically for women darts players. Ranking is based on players' performances in the PDC Women's Series tournaments.

The top eight players will receive a starting ticket to the Women's World Matchplay tournament. The top two players may compete in the PDC World Darts Championship.

The number one player on the list will receive an invitation to the Grand Slam of Darts.

DID YOU KNOW?

Luke Littler narrowly missed the chance to play Fallon Sherrock in the second round of the 2025 PDC World Darts Championship. Instead, he played Ryan Meikle, beating him 3–1. Meikle had defeated Sherrock in their match 3–2, preventing her from facing 'The Nuke'.

SPOTLIGHT ON
TRINA GULLIVER

Trina Gulliver, born in 1968, was the first winner of the first Women's Darts Championship, introduced in 2001 by the BDO. Between 2001 and 2007, she dominated the women's game, winning seven consecutive world titles. Known as 'Golden Girl', Trina has, as of 2025, won ten Women's World Professional Darts Championships and six World Masters, making her the world's most successful women's darts player of all time. In 2003, she was named BBC Midlands Sports Personality of the Year. She was also awarded an MBE in 2013 for her services to the sport of darts and her charitable work.

SPOTLIGHT ON BEAU GREAVES

Beau Greaves, was at the top of the PDC Women's Series rankings in 2023 and 2024. At just 24 years old, in 2025 she was ranked as the women's world number one in WDF events. However, if Beau wants to defend her WDF world title, she can't play top players like Luke Littler at the next PDC World Darts Championship because of the rule (named the Tomlin order) of 1997 made following the BDO/WDC split.

REACHING FOR THE TOP!

In 2025, after his 2024 World Darts Championship win, Luke Littler reached world number two in the PDC Order of Merit ranking system, behind Luke Humphries, the number one darts player in the world. Number two is an incredible achievement considering that Littler had only been playing at a professional level for just over one year before reaching that level, and the ranking system is based on the results over a two-year period. With everything to play for, Littler wants to reach for the number one spot!

"I know Luke Humphries, I said it earlier on, he's got a lot to defend so maybe I could get to world number one. Yeah. Obviously, we all know Luke's got the capability to go, and well, not retain everything, but to go and defend all the prize money that he won two years back, but I'm hoping that I can either stop him or other players can stop him, so I can get to number one."

– Luke Littler speaking about his dream of becoming the world's number one darts player

TIMELINE OF LITTLER'S CAREER HIGHLIGHTS

2021
WDF Irish Open Men's Winner

2021
3 x JDC Advanced Tours

2021
5 x WDF Youth Wins

2021
JDC MVG Masters 9 Darter

2022

Selected for England Men's Team

2022

3 x JDC Advanced Tours

2022

JDC Super 16 Winner

2022

WDF Isle of Man Youth Winner

2022

WDF Men's World Championships – last 16

2022

WDF Welsh Classic Youth Winner

2022
WDF Welsh Open Youth and Men's Winner

2022
Selected for JDC England A Team

2022
Romanian Classics Winner

2022
ADC Grand Slam Liverpool Winner

2022
WDF Boys World Masters Champion

2022
JDC World Champion

2023
UK Open Qualifier

2023
JDC Super 16 Winner – events 1, 3, and 4

2023
JDC Tour Card Holder

2023
Isle of Man Youth Grand Prix Winner

2023
Isle of Man Mixed Pairs Champion

2023
Isle of Man Classic Men's Winner – hitting a nine-darter en route

2023

PDC Development Tour 20 Nine-Dart Finish

2023

PDC Development Tour 3, 5, 16 and 20 Winner

2023

JDC Advanced Tour 5, 6, 8, 10 and 12 Winner

2023

MODUS Super Series 3 Week 10 Champion

2023

MODUS Super Series 3 Champion of Champions

2023

MODUS Super Series 4 Week 8 Champion

2023

Cheshire Open Men's Pairs Winner

2023

MODUS Super Series 4 Champion of Champions – first champion to defend their title

2023

ADC Vault Winner

2023

WDF British Classic Men's Event Champion

2023

JDC World Cup Bronze Medallist

2023

MVG Masters Champion

2023

WDF Gibraltar Juniors Open Champion

2023

WDF Gibraltar Open Men's Champion

2023

WDF Gibraltar Open Youth Champion

2023

WDF British Open Champion

2023

PDC World Youth Champion

2023

JDC Number 1

2024
PDC World Darts Championship Finalist

2024
PDC Bahrain Darts Masters Champion

2024
PDC Belgian Darts Open Champion

2024
PDC Austrian Darts Open Champion

2024
Premier League Champion

2024
Poland Darts Masters Champion

2024
PDC Players Championship 15 Winner

2024
World Series of Darts Champion

2024
Grand Slam of Darts Champion

2025
World Darts Championship Winner

2025
UK Open Darts Winner

2025
European Tour Belgian Darts Open Winner

LUKE IN 2025 AND GOING FORWARD...

As he progresses through 2025 on the professional darts circuit, Luke is living up to his name 'The Nuke', stunning the world with his remarkable talent, his fast-paced games and dedication to the sport that he has loved since he was a toddler.

Luke's ambition is to win every major darts title at least once, although beating former world champion Phil Taylor, one of his darting heroes and a great inspiration to him, does pose a huge challenge. However, if he carries on playing like he is, displaying incredible skills, and great drive and focus way beyond his years, then this young rising star is definitely on the right path to achieving his dream, and maybe even surpassing his hero's record-breaking form. Could he become the darting world's number one champion? Watch this space...

"I have certainly broken the rules and records already but I know if my game is there I can beat even more records. I think I am daring to dream now. I am only three wins away."

– Luke Littler on reaching the quarter finals of the 2024 PDC World Darts Championships.

> "It was my dad who told me to stop playing football and that my darts were more important. I just looked at him and said, 'I love football'. That's every kid's dream. Luckily, it has paid off."

– Luke Littler on choosing darts over football. A big THANK YOU to Luke's dad – your son is setting the world of darts on fire!

LUKE'S 2025 PREMIER LEAGUE DARTS JOURNEY

We already know how good Littler is and 2025 is really turning out to be his year as he continues to add wins to his tournament calendar.

The Premier League is no exception, with unprecedented wins from The Nuke. The 18-year-old champion defeated big-name players Stephen Bunting (6–1), Nathan Aspinall (6–4) and Luke Humphries (6–3) to finish top of the league table on Night 16, securing him a place in the final play-offs alongside Gerwyn Price, Nathan Aspinall and Luke Humphries. His win against Bunting saw him break the record for points (45) in the Premier League season.

Despite his best efforts, sadly Littler was beaten 11–8 by Luke Humphries in a closely fought match. But this is not the end of the road for the young champion from Warrington. Big-hearted and gracious in defeat, Luke is sure to up his game in his next tournament as he continues to break records and show the world what a superstar he is!

SPOTLIGHT ON
PHIL TAYLOR

Phil Taylor, known as 'The Power', is arguably the world's greatest darts player. He is the 14-times winner of the PDC World Darts Championship between 1995 and 2013, with a previous two wins in 1990 and 1992 before the split with the BDO, and 16-time winner of the PDC World Matchplay between 1995 and 2017. Over the span of his darts career, Phil has won 214 professional tournaments!

Now retired (he put down his darts in 2018, aside from a brief return to the sport in 2022–24 for the Senior Darts tour), this superstar still had time to meet with his number one fan. Luke was bowled over to come face-to-face with his hero. I'm sure Phil had plenty of great advice to pass on to the young darts prodigy as they sat down to a fun game of Jenga. He graciously lost to Luke in a match that lasted 3 minutes and 40 seconds. 'The Power' was defeated by 'The Nuke'!

"I knew that I was going to have to be at my very best to block out the noise and knock over such an incredible opponent ... Phil is such a towering player who has set the bar so high in his amazing career, so it feels great to have kept a steady hand and secured a win against a true legend."

– Luke Littler on his Jenga game with the legendary Phil Taylor

"It was a high-stakes match. I thought I might've had the edge with experience, but fair play to Luke, he held his nerve, and I crumbled! He really knows how to take his opponent down, piece by piece. I'm sure we'll continue to see him make the right moves and reach new heights."

– Phil Taylor on his game of Jenga with Luke Littler

SPOTLIGHT ON
RAYMOND VAN BARNEVELD

Dutch superstar and former world number one darts player Raymond van Barneveld, known as 'Barney', is one of Luke's darting idols, and one of the sport's most successful players. Born in 1967, the five-time world champion is one of only three players to achieve five World Championship titles and the first player to achieve a nine-dart finish in both the 2006 Premier League and the 2009 PDC World Darts Championship.

Luke was thrilled to be playing his hero in the 2024 PDC World Darts Championship. Ahead of the match, Luke shared a video on his social media platforms of himself as a child imitating this legend – after hitting the target on a real dartboard, Luke raised his arms in a Barney-style celebration!

"I can't believe it. He just beat a legend. I don't know what to say. He used to watch Barney when he was three and he's just beat him — it's crazy!"

– Luke Littler's dad after Luke defeated Barneveld in the last 16 of the 2024 PDC World Darts Championship

SPOTLIGHT ON
MICHAEL VAN GERWEN

Michael 'Mighty Mike' van Gerwen is another of Luke's heroes and a three-time world champion. Born in 1989, this Dutch superstar was only 17 when he made his meteoric rise in the sport, winning the 2006 BDO World Masters. He was victorious again in 2012 when he won the World Grand Prix, and then went on win three World Championships in 2014, 2017 and 2019. He claimed the world number one spot for eight years during this period.

Luke and Gerwen are now sporting rivals, competing for the major darts tournament titles. On the circuit in 2024, they came head-to-head in many championships, battling for the top spot. Then came the historic moment in January 2025 when both players met the ultimate challenge of defeating some of the world's best players to earn a place in the finals of the PDC World Darts Championship. In an epic, electric match, The Nuke defeated his hero Mighty Mike 7 sets to 3.

THROWING FOR FUN!

Whether you are playing darts with a view to becoming a professional on the world stage, or you just want to have fun with your mates, darts is an accessible sport. Look out for clubs at your school or in your local community. Or if you have space at home – check with your adults in charge first – you could set up a playing area and stage matches with your friends and family. Remember, Luke started playing at home and look where he is now!

If you want to start with a shorter version of the standard 501 game, you could play 301. This is essentially the same game, but you have to score fewer points (200 fewer, if you are practising your mental maths!) in each leg. It's a good way to practise your throwing techniques and to find a comfortable standing stance and dart grip. You can also practise your maths skills by working out how you can reduce your score from 301 to 0. All this will help you build up your confidence and help you develop your own techniques and strategies.

The darts game called Cricket is another fun way to enjoy the game. The objective is to hit each of the numbers 15 to 20, plus the bullseye, three times to 'close' them. Once you've closed a number, you can score by hitting the closed numbers as many times as possible before your opponent closes the same number. The player or team with the highest score when all the numbers are closed wins.

Check out the picture here to see how to make your own score card. The central column lists the numbers 20 down to 15 and the bullseye. Add two columns either side for each player or team. The outside column is for recording your scores and the inner one is for closing out.

		LETS PLAY DARTS!		
		vs.		
	_01	CRICKET	_01	
		20		
		19		
		18		
		17		
		16		
		15		
		Bull		

Players take it in turns to throw three darts. You can aim for any of the sections (15 to 20 or the bullseye), but you can potentially earn more points if you close out the higher numbers first.

Use the marks shown here to keep track of how many times you and your opponent have hit a number or the bullseye. The goal is to have an X with a circle around it by each number to show that you have closed it.

One slash / = 1 hit

Another slash to make X = 2 hits

A circled ⊗ = 3 hits

> **For the numbers 15 to 20,
> hitting the outer double ring = 2 hits**
>
> **For the numbers 15 to 20,
> hitting the inner triple ring = 3 hits**
>
> **For the bullseye,
> hitting the outer ring = 1 hit**
>
> **For the bullseye,
> hitting the inner ring = 2 hits**

When you have three hits, you have closed that number. If your opponent hasn't already closed that number, you can score points on it on your turn. Until your opponent closes the number, every time you hit it, you score points. Once both players have closed a number, points can no longer be scored on it.

For example, if you close out 20 first, you can score 20 points for a single hit, 40 points for a double and 60 points for a triple until your opponent also closes the 20.

This scoring applies to all the numbers 15 through to 20:

- a single hit is worth the number's value

- a double hit is worth two times the number's value

- a triple hit is worth three times the number's value

- the outer bullseye = 25 points

- the inner bullseye = 50 points

To close the bullseye, you can either hit the outer ring three times or hit the outer ring once and the inner ring once.

Total the scores in the outer columns once all the numbers and the bullseye are closed by both players. The highest score wins the game.

A BRIEF HISTORY OF DARTS

Most references to the origins of darts trace back to the Middle Ages and to archery. There are stories of soldiers passing the time between battles by throwing broken arrow stubs at upturned wine barrels to see who could get closest to the centre.

In 19th century France, people played a game called 'flechettes', which means 'small arrows'. This is the first historic reference to a game like darts. Small wooden arrows with a metal tip and flights made from bird feathers were thrown at targets.

In the UK, it is thought that darts started out as a fairground game. By the early 20th century, there are records of darts being played as a pub game. The game grew in popularity and local leagues were set up. After World War One, a National Darts Association (NDA) was formed to regulate the game and establish the rules.

By the 1930s, darts had become a popular recreational game across the UK. Soldiers were issued with darts during World War Two so they could play during their downtime, and by the end of the war the game had established itself in many different countries.

The original NDA was taken over by the British Darts Organisation (BDO) in the 1970s. The 1970s and 1980s were the decades of TV darts – the televised games were hugely popular, opening the sport to a wider audience. Top darts players became household names. Fans would flock to watch live staged tournaments, sporting fancy dress costumes and wearing the colours of their favourite players.

Though there was a slump in televised games in the 1990s, the game of darts was here to stay. The newly independent PDC brought an exciting level of professionalism and entertainment to the sport, with its packed annual calendar of tournaments and multiple opportunities for darts players of all ages to play at a professional level and win big money prizes.

Players have adopted walk-on tunes, playing their favourite songs as they walk up to the oche for their matches. This pumps their fans in the crowd up into a cheering frenzy! The songs reflect the players' personalities and help them connect with their fans, as well as enhancing the atmosphere and the crowd's experience of the game.

The televised razzamatazz of the sport has increased the popularity of the game, attracting big sponsorships and prizes, and has opened the sport up to wider, global audiences. The top darts players have become sporting heroes around the world, with dedicated fans following all of their matches and celebrating their victories in colourful and wacky fancy dress costumes!

TOP PLAYERS' WALK-ON SONGS

Luke Littler:
Greenlight
by Pitbull

Stephen Bunting:
Titanium
by David Guetta

Michael van Gerwen:
Seven Nation Army
by The White Stripes

Chris Dobey:
Let's Get Ready to Rumble
by PJ & Duncan aka Ant & Dec

Luke Humphries:
I Predict a Riot
by Kaiser Chiefs

Michael Smith:
Shut Up and Dance
by Walk the Moon

Rob Cross:
I Don't Wanna Wait
by David Guetta and OneRepublic

Damon Heta:
My Songs Know What You Did in the Dark
by Fall Out Boy

Nathan Aspinall:
Mr Brightside
by The Killers

Raymond van Barneveld:
Eye of the Tiger
by Survivor

Fallon Sherrock:
Last Friday Night (T.G.I.F.)
by Katy Perry

Beau Greaves:
Rockin' All Over the World
by Status Quo

Tina Gulliver:
You Sexy Thing
by Hot Chocolate

Lisa Ashton:
On a Mission
by Gabriella Cilmi

Deta Hedman:
Hot, Hot, Hot
by Buster Poindexter

Mikuru Suzuki:
Baby Shark
by Pinkfong

WOMEN IN DARTS

It wasn't really until the beginning of the 21st century that women darts players began to be recognized in a professional capacity. Until then, although there were many great female players, the sport was dominated by male players, with more televised matches and exposure, bigger money prizes and more professional opportunities for men.

In 2001, the BDO staged the Women's World Championship for the first time. The PDC didn't open regular spots for women players in their World Darts Championship until 2018. They can now compete alongside male players. The PDC doesn't yet have a separate world championship for women, which many women players are unhappy about, but they did launch the Women's Series in 2020, which includes female-only tournaments that give the top women players an opportunity to take part in some of the PDC's biggest tournaments, such as the Grand Slam of Darts and the World Darts Championship.

There is still a long way to go in terms of equal exposure and prize money for women in the sport, but things are slowly improving, and there are now more opportunities than ever for young girls and women to play the game at a professional level.

WOMEN PLAYERS STATS AND RECORDS

- Trina Gulliver won the first female darts players BDO World Championship in 2001.
- Fallon Sherrock won two of her matches in the 2019 PDC World Darts Championship.
- In 2020, Lisa Ashton was the first female darts player to win a PDC Tour Card at the Qualifying School, which allowed her to compete for two years on the professional tour against other worldclass players.
- In 2023, Beau Greaves finished top of the Women's Series Order of Merit.

LUKE LITTLER TIMELINE

2007

Born on 21 January at Warrington Hospital in Warrington, UK.

2008

Aged 18 months, began playing with magnetic darts.

2011

Starting playing with real darts and dartboard.

2013

Moved from Runcorn to Warrington.

2016

Won an under-14s tournament at St Helens Darts Academy.

2018

Won the St Helens Open under-13s competition.

2019

Won the England Youth Grand Prix.

Won the Youth Isle of Man Masters, his first WDF title.

Won his first JDC title at the third Super 16 event, qualifying for the finals.

2020

Won the Youth Isle of Man Masters title for the second time.

Signed up for the Target Elite programme and signed to ZXF Sports Management.

Won his first JDC Tour title.

2021

Won the JDC Super 16 boys' title.

Won five WDF Youth titles and became England's Youth Open champion.

Won the Irish Open, his first senior title. This qualified him for the men's WDF World Championship.

Threw his first televised nine-dart finish at the MVG Masters in Gibraltar.

2022

Debuted at the WDF World Championship. Went through to the last 16.

Won the JDC Super 16.

Won the Welsh Open and the Romanian Classic, his second and third senior winning titles.

Representing England, won gold medals in the WDF Europe Youth Cup in the boys' team, pairs and singles events and the men's team event.

Won the WDF World Masters Boys title.

Won the JDC World Championship.

2023

Won the JDC Super 16 title.

Won the JDC World Championship.

Won senior titles in the British Open, British Classic, Gibraltar Open and Isle of Man Classic.

Debuted in the UK Open, where he reached the fourth round.

Secured a PDC Tour Card for 2024 and a place in the 2024 PDC World Darts Championship after finishing as runner-up on the PDC Tour Order of Merit.

Played in the Modus Super Series, becoming the first player to defend the Champions Week title.

Won the PDC World Youth Championship, becoming the youngest-ever winner.

2024

Defeated in the final of the PDC World Darts Championship.

Won the Bahrain Darts Masters.

Won the Poland Darts Masters.

Won the Players Championship 1, 15 and 20 on the ProTour.

Won the Belgian and Austrian Darts Opens on the European Tour.

Won the Premier League.

Won the World Series Finals.

Won the Grand Slam of Darts.

Number 2 in the PDC Order of Merit.

Number 1 in the World Series of Darts Order of Merit.

Number 3 in the EuroTour Order of Merit.

Named BBC Young Sports Personality of the Year.

Runner-up to Keely Hodgkinson in the BBC Sports Personality of the Year.

2025

Won the PDC World Darts Championship just before his 18th birthday.

Runner up in the final of the Premier League at the O2 Arena.

BEYOND 2025

2025 is proving to be a sensational year for Luke. Like his darts, Luke is hitting the mark as he continues to take the darting world by storm. This young star from Warrington takes every game and every tournament seriously. From the get-go, Littler sets out to win. He doesn't shy away from hard work.

To stay at the top of his game, Littler needs to keep up his practice. His sunny nature and resilience shine through, even in the face of his gruelling and exhausting tournament schedules. Every time he steps up to the oche, he aims to give his best performance, not only for himself but also for his fans.

To be a sporting star takes a lot of work and Luke certainly has a fantastic work ethic, as well as determination and drive by the bucketload! Being a star in such a fast-paced sport means you must roll with your failures as well as your successes. You have to pick yourself up, learn from your mistakes and keep on going. You have to be humble and gracious in defeat. That is not always an easy thing to do, but it helps when you have plenty of support.

On top of the support Luke receives from his family, he can seek advice and encouragement from his darts colleagues. Players share a lot of camaraderie and banter. The interactions on the oche before and after a match are good-humoured and respectful. Win or lose, players shake hands or hug at the end of a game and are supportive of each other.

For such a young and newly professional player, and for someone who has become an overnight sensation, Luke has been incredible at striking a happy balance between his sporting fame and his home life. As 'The Nuke', he loves the exciting world of darts and all the challenges it brings, and as the young lad Luke, he loves his everyday life with his family and friends.

The world of darts is Luke's oyster. This young star is still at the beginning of his career and has so much more to offer the sport. Luke has the skill and potential to win many more titles and keep breaking records. Good luck Luke. We're watching with anticipation.

IT'S ALL IN THE NAME

Check out these awesome darts players' nicknames. Cover the players' names and see if you can match the nickname to the player!

The Nuke	Luke Littler
Beau 'n' Arrow	Beau Greaves
Cool Hand Luke	Luke Humphries
Mighty Mike	Michael van Gerwen
The Queen of the Palace	Fallon Sherrock
The Power	Phil Taylor
Golden Girl	Trina Gulliver
Barney	Raymond van Barneveld
Miracle	Mikuru Suzuki
The Bullet	Stephen Bunting
The Storm	Sandy Hudson

The Iceman	Gerwyn Price
Super Sue	Sue Edwards
The Asp	Nathan Aspinall
Smiley	Talisa Zwart
The Machine	James Wade
The Wright Stuff	Tricia Wright
Snakebite	Peter Wright
Legend	Patricia Farrell
Voltage	Rob Cross
Bambie	Mieke de Boer
Jackpot	Adrian Lewis
OB	Maria O'Brien
The Ferret	Jonny Clayton
The Party Starter	Lynsey McDonald
The Flying Scotsman	Gary Anderson
Ice Cube	Julie Gore
Dutch Destroyer	Vincent van der Voort
Ice Baby	Irena Armstrong

WORLD CHAMPION DARTS QUIZ

Here's your chance to test your darts knowledge and show what a superfan you are. Step up to the oche and take the quiz or play it with your mates to find your own darts master! Who will hit 180?

All you need is a pen and paper. Each player starts with 180 points. Each time you answer a question correctly, deduct the point(s) for that question. Make a score card to keep track of everyone's points. The winner is the first player to reach zero or the person with the lowest score by the end of all the questions. If there is a tie, the first player to answer the knockout tiebreaker question correctly wins the title and the trophy.

If you are playing with a larger group and you want to make things a little more competitive, introduce knockout rounds to eliminate players who have answered the fewest questions correctly as you go. Before you play, decide how many players will be knocked out after how many rounds.

Make your own trophy! Copy this picture onto a piece of card. Colour your trophy. At the end of the quiz, write the winner's name on the cup and hand them their prize!

QUESTIONS

ROUND 1 (Score 1 point per question)

1. When was Luke Littler born?

2. When Luke and his family left Runcorn, where did they move to?

3. How old was Luke when he started playing darts?

4. How old was Luke when he scored his first 180?

5. What is the name of the darts academy that Luke joined?

6. Why is Luke nicknamed, 'The Nuke'?

7. What football team does Luke support?

8. What rugby team does Luke support?

9. What's Luke's favourite post-match takeaway?

10. On social media, what is Luke's rapid rise to fame known as?

ROUND 2 (Score 2 points per question)

1. In what year did Luke win the WDF England Youth Grand Prix?

2. Which specialist supplier of darts products sponsors Luke?

3. In 2021, Luke won his first senior title. At which tournament did he achieve this?

4. His first senior title meant Luke qualified for one of the top tournaments in the sport. What tournament was this?

5. In 2022, Luke was part of the team that won a gold medal in which Cup competition?

6. At which major PDC event did Luke make his debut in 2023?

7. In 2023, how many titles did Luke win in the PDC Development Tour series?

8. Luke came second in the 2023 Development Tour Order of Merit. What did this qualify him for?

9. Which player did Luke defeat in the finals of the 2023 PDC World Youth Championship?

10. Luke defeated his childhood hero, and five-time world champion, in the fourth round of the 2024 PDC World Darts Championship. Who was this player?

ROUND 3 (Score 3 points per question)

1. Name the number one world champion who Luke defeated in the semi-final of the 2024 PDC World Darts Championship?

2. Who did Luke lose to in the final of the 2024 PDC World Darts Championship and what was the score?

3. How many titles did Luke win in 2024?

4. In 2024, what was Luke's PDC ranking?

5. How many nine-dart finishes did Luke make in 2024?

6. Luke made his first televised nine-dart finish in the 2024 Bahrain Darts Masters. Who was he playing against when he made it?

7. In 2024, in which tournament did Luke earn fifth place on the PDC Order of Merit?

8. In the final match of the PDC World Darts Championship, the match is played to the best of how many sets? And the winner is the first player to win how many of these sets?

9. What are the 32 highest ranked players on the PDC Order of Merit allowed to do in the PDC World Darts Championship?

10. Who did Luke defeat in the finals of the 2025 PDC World Darts Championship and what was the score?

ROUND 4 (Score 3 points per question)

1. Who was the number one seeded player at the start of the 2025 PDC World Darts Championship?

2. Luke won how much prize money for being the winner of the 2025 PDC World Darts Championship?

3. What is the name of the prestigious PDC World Darts Championship trophy and what was the profession of the person it was named after?

4. When Luke Littler became the youngest world champion in PDC history, he beat the record previously held by which player?

5. Luke was the first darts player to be given a particular award in 2024. What was the award?

6. In 2024, Luke hit a record-breaking number of 180s, the highest number of any professional player that year. How many did he hit?

7. What do WDF and PDC stand for?

8. Which three PDC tournaments make up the Triple Crown?

9. Who is the worldwide governing body of the sport of darts?

10. Which PDC tournaments are for women players only?

QUARTER-FINAL (Score 3 points per question)

1. What does a 'bed and breakfast' refer to in a game of darts?

2. What does a 'nine-dart finish' or 'nine-dart leg' refer to in a game of darts?

3. How many players are granted a PDC Tour Card every year?

4. How many main PDC Order of Merit rankings are there in the sport?

5. Who was the first winner of the first Women's Darts Championship, introduced in 2001 by the BDO?

6. What is the name of the rule that says players cannot compete in both the WDF World Championship and the PDC World Darts Championship in the same year?

7. How far from the wall that the dartboard is mounted on must the oche (or throw line) be placed?

8. In a game of 501, what must a player do to finish a leg?

9. How many points does a player score if they throw a single 11, a double 17 and a triple 12?

10. With three darts, what would you need to hit to score 180?

SEMI-FINAL (Score 4 points per question)

1. According to official darts rules, what parts must a dart feature?

2. What darts does Luke use?

3. Luke's darts are made of what material (90% of the dart)?

4. Why does Luke prefer to play with darts that have longer points?

5. Most references to the origins of the game of darts date to which period of history?

6. What were the first darts?

7. What is Luke's walk-on song?

8. What event was Luke attending with his dad when he heard the song that he later adopted as his walk-on song?

9. Name three of Luke's darts player heroes.

10. When was the sport first televised in the UK?

FINAL (Score 5 points per question)

1. What was the former name of the Professional Darts Corporation (PDC)?

2. Where is the PDC World Darts Championship held every year?

3. What PDC tournament is held annually between February and May?

4. Who was the first female player to win a match in the PDC World Darts Championship in 2020?

5. In 2025, who was ranked as the women's world number one in WDF events?

6. As of 2025, who is arguably the world's greatest darts player of all time?

7. What is Phil Taylor's darts nickname?

8. How many professional tournaments did Phil Taylor win over the course of his darts career?

9. Who was the first player to achieve a nine-dart finish in both the 2006 Premier League and the 2009 PDC World Darts Championship?

10. For how many years did Luke's sporting rival and hero, Michael van Gerwen, hold the world number one spot?

Tie breaker:
Where did Luke go to school?

ANSWERS

ROUND 1 (Score 1 point per question)

1 Q: When was Luke Littler born?
   A: 21 January 2007.

2 Q: When Luke and his family left Runcorn, where did they move to?
   A: Warrington, Cheshire, UK.

3 Q: How old was Luke when he started playing darts?
   A: 18 months old.

4 Q: How old was Luke when he scored his first 180?
   A: Six years old.

5 Q: What is the name of the darts academy that Luke joined?
   A: St Helens Darts Academy.

6 **Q:** Why is Luke nicknamed, 'The Nuke'?
   A: Luke's darts nickname reflects his explosive talent and his ability to dominate matches.

7 **Q:** What football team does Luke support?
   A: Manchester United.

8 **Q:** What rugby team does Luke support?
   A: The Warrington Wolves.

9 **Q:** What's Luke's favourite post-match takeaway?
   A: Doner kebab with lettuce and loads of mayo.

10 **Q:** On social media, what is Luke's rapid rise to fame known as?
   A: Littlermania.

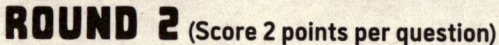

ROUND 2 (Score 2 points per question)

1 **Q:** In what year did Luke win the WDF England Youth Grand Prix?
A: 2019, when he was 12 years old.

2 **Q:** Which specialist supplier of darts products sponsors Luke?
A: Target.

3 **Q:** In 2021, Luke won his first senior title. At which tournament did he achieve this?
A: The Irish Open.

4 **Q:** His first senior title meant Luke qualified for one of the top tournaments in the sport. What tournament was this?
A: The 2022 WDF World Darts Championship.

5 **Q:** In 2022, Luke was part of the team that won a gold medal in which Cup competition?
A: 2022 WDF Europe Cup.

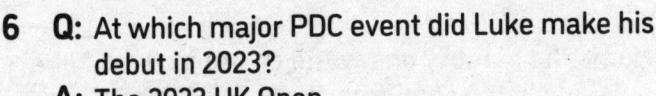

6 **Q:** At which major PDC event did Luke make his debut in 2023?
A: The 2023 UK Open.

7 **Q:** In 2023, how many titles did Luke win in the PDC Development Tour series?
A: He won five titles.

8 **Q:** Luke came second in the 2023 Development Tour Order of Merit. What did this qualify him for?
A: This qualified him to play in the 2024 PDC World Darts championship.

9 **Q:** Which player did Luke defeat in the finals of the 2023 PDC World Youth Championship?
A: Gian van Veen.

10 **Q:** Luke defeated his childhood hero, and five-time world champion, in the fourth round of the 2024 PDC World Darts Championship. Who was this player?
A: Raymond van Barneveld.

ROUND 3 (Score 3 points per question)

1 Q: Name the number one world champion who Luke defeated in the semi-final of the 2024 PDC World Darts Championship?
A: Rob Cross.

2 Q: Who did Luke lose to in the final of the 2024 PDC World Darts Championship and what was the score?
A: Luke Humphries. He defeated Littler in 7 sets to 4.

3 Q: How many titles did Luke win in 2024?
A: He won 10 titles.

4 Q: In 2024, what was Luke's PDC ranking?
A: He was ranked fourth.

5 Q: How many nine-dart finishes did Luke make in 2024?
A: He made four nine-dart finishes.

6 Q: Luke made his first televised nine-dart finish in the 2024 Bahrain Darts Masters. Who was he playing against when he made it?
A: He was playing Nathan Aspinall.

7 Q: In 2024, in which tournament did Luke earn fifth place on the PDC Order of Merit?
A: The Grand Slam of Darts.

8 Q: In the final match of the PDC World Darts Championship, the match is played to the best of how many sets? And the winner is the first player to win how many of these sets?
A: The final match is played to the best of 13 sets, and the winner is the first player to win seven sets.

9 Q: What are the 32 highest ranked players on the PDC Order of Merit allowed to do in the PDC World Darts Championship?
A: They are allowed to skip round one and go straight into playing in round two.

10 Q: Who did Luke defeat in the finals of the 2025 PDC World Darts Championship and what was the score?
A: Michael van Gerwen and the score was 7 sets to 3.

ROUND 4 (Score 3 points per question)

1 Q: Who was the number one seeded player at the start of the 2025 PDC World Darts Championship?
A: Luke Humphries.

2 Q: Luke won how much prize money for being the winner of the 2025 PDC World Darts Championship?
A: £500,000.

3 Q: What is the name of the prestigious PDC World Darts Championship trophy and what was the profession of the person it was named after?
A: The trophy is called the Sid Waddell Trophy, and it is named after Sid Waddell, the legendary commentator who was the voice of the sport for almost four decades.

4 Q: When Luke Littler became the youngest world champion in PDC history, he beat the record previously held by which player?
A: The record was previously held by Michael van Gerwen, who was 24 years old when he won the tournament in 2014.

5 Q: Luke was the first darts player to be given a particular award in 2024. What was the award?
A: The BBC Young Sports Personality of the Year.

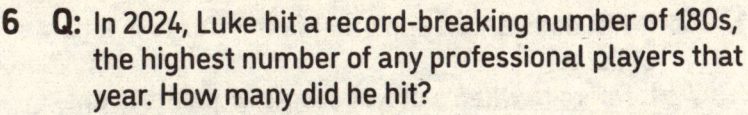

6 **Q:** In 2024, Luke hit a record-breaking number of 180s, the highest number of any professional players that year. How many did he hit?
A: He hit 836 in total.

7 **Q:** What do WDF and PDC stand for?
A: WDF is World Darts Federation and PDC is Professional Darts Corporation.

8 **Q:** Which three PDC tournaments make up the Triple Crown?
A: The World Darts Championship, the Premier League Darts competitions and the World Matchplay are the Triple Crown, being the most prestigious and biggest darts tournaments in the world.

9 **Q:** Who is the worldwide governing body of the sport of darts?
A: The World Darts Federation (WDF).

10 **Q:** Which PDC tournaments are for women players only?
A: The Women's Series and the Women's Matchplay.

QUARTER-FINAL (Score 3 points per question)

1 Q: What does a 'bed and breakfast' refer to in a game of darts?
A: It refers to when a player scores 26 points in one visit, usually with a single 20, a single 5 and a single 1. A very, very long time ago, staying at a bed and breakfast would have only cost you two shillings and six pence (two and six)!

2 Q: What does a 'nine-dart finish' or 'nine-dart leg' refer to in a game of darts?
A: The perfect leg of darts using just nine darts to get from 501 to zero.

3 Q: How many players are granted a PDC Tour Card every year?
A: 128 players.

4 Q: How many main PDC Order of Merit rankings are there in the sport?
A: There are eight main rankings which grant ranked status and allow players to qualify for the top professional tournaments.

5 Q: Who was the first winner of the first Women's Darts Championship, introduced in 2001 by the BDO?
A: Trina Gulliver, who as of 2025 is the world's most successful women's darts player of all time.

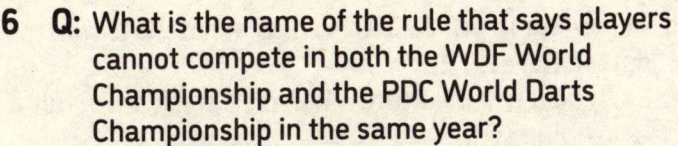

6 Q: What is the name of the rule that says players cannot compete in both the WDF World Championship and the PDC World Darts Championship in the same year?
A: The 1997 Tomlin Order.

7 Q: How far from the wall that the dartboard is mounted on must the oche (or throw line) be placed?
A: 2.37 metres.

8 Q: In a game of 501, what must a player do to finish a leg?
A: The player must reduce their score to zero by throwing a double on their last throw.

9 Q: How many points does a player score if they throw a single 11, a double 17 and a triple 12?
A: They score a total of 81 points.

10 Q: With three darts, what would you need to hit to score 180?
A: You would need to hit the triple 20 with each dart.

SEMI-FINAL (Score 4 points per question)

1 **Q:** According to official darts rules, what parts must a dart feature?
A: Each dart must feature a barrel, a stem and a flight.

2 **Q:** What darts does Luke use?
A: He uses Target's Luke Littler Gen 1 Darts.

3 **Q:** Luke's darts are made of what material (90% of the dart)?
A: His darts are made of 90% tungsten.

4 **Q:** Why does Luke prefer to play with darts that have longer points?
A: A longer point covers less of the target on the board which allows him to fit one or two more darts in the same segment, giving him a better chance of hitting higher scores in the double, triple and bullseye segments.

5 **Q:** Most references to the origins of the game of darts date to which period of history?
A: The Middle Ages.

6 **Q:** What were the first darts?
A: They were arrow stubs, broken from battles, which soldiers used to throw at upturned wine barrels.

7 **Q:** What is Luke's walk-on song?
A: 'Greenlight' by Pitbull, featuring Flo Rider and Lunchmoney Lewis.

8 **Q:** What event was Luke attending with his dad when he heard the song that he later adopted as his walk-on song?
A: He was at a WWE event, Wrestlemania, in the USA.

9 **Q:** Name three of Luke's darts player heroes.
A: Phil Taylor, Raymond van Barneveld and Michael van Gerwen.

10 **Q:** When was the sport first televised in the UK?
A: Darts was first televised in 1937.

FINAL (Score 5 points per question)

1 Q: What was the former name of the Professional Darts Corporation (PDC)?
A: The World Darts Council (WDC) that was established in 1992 after the split from the BDO.

2 Q: Where is the PDC World Darts Championship held every year?
A: Alexandra Palace in London.

3 Q: What PDC tournament is held annually between February and May?
A: Premier League Darts, which is held as a series of weekly leagues.

4 Q: Who was the first female player to win a match in the PDC World Darts Championship in 2020?
A: Fallon Sherrock.

5 Q: In 2025, who was ranked as the women's world number one in WDF events?
A: Beau Greaves.

6 **Q:** As of 2025, who is arguably the world's greatest darts player of all time?
A: Phil Taylor, 14-time winner of the PDC World Darts Championship between 1995 and 2013, with a previous two wins in 1990 and 1992 before the split with the BDO, and 16-time winner of the PDC World Matchplay between 1995 and 2017.

7 **Q:** What is Phil Taylor's darts nickname?
A: The Power.

8 **Q:** How many professional tournaments did Phil Taylor win over the course of his darts career?
A: 214.

9 **Q:** Who was the first player to achieve a nine-dart finish in both the 2006 Premier League and the 2009 PDC World Darts Championship?
A: Dutch superstar Raymond van Barneveld.

10 **Q:** For how many years did Luke's sporting rival and hero, Michael van Gerwen, hold the world number one spot?
A: Eight years, between 2012 and 2019.

Tie breaker:
Q: Where did Luke go to school?
A: Padgate Academy, Warrington, England.